An o

CW01431196

SOUTH LONDON

Written by
EMMY WATTS

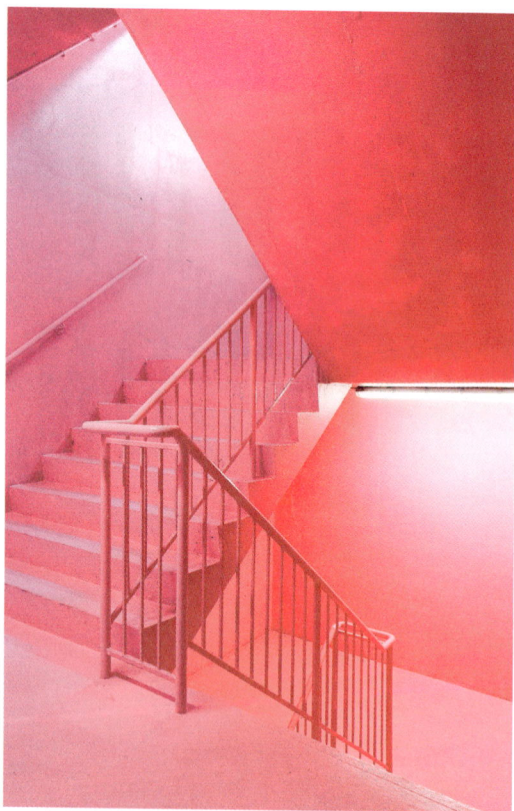

Bold Tendencies (no.68)

INFORMATION IS DEAD.
LONG LIVE OPINION.

What's the point of this book? You can find out everything about south London online.

But you don't need to know *everything* – you only need to know the very best. Life is already too full of information. This is our lively, compact and unashamedly opinionated guide to *only* the greatest things to do south of the river. Why should you listen to us, a small indie publisher based in Hackney? Because we live and breathe *all* of London (and the editor of this is book happens to be a true south Londoner). Oh, and south London is the BIGGEST bit of town, hence this is our biggest guide yet.

Iyouall (no.30)

Opposite: The Camberwell Arms (no.5)

Brockwell Lido (no.50)
Opposite: Richmond Park (no.47)

Southbank Centre (no.60)
Opposite: White Cube (no.57)

THE BEAUTIFUL SOUTH

What springs to mind when you think of south London? Is it the wide-reaching stretches of green space? Perhaps it's the booming gastronomic scene that orbits around the capital's oldest food market. Or maybe your first thought is for the region's rich cultural heritage, encompassing everything from majestic medieval palaces (no.63) to a Victorian amusement park inhabited by anatomically dubious clay dinosaurs (no.46).

If any of the above rings true, this book is for you. It's an unabashed celebration of everything that's great about south London, from the breathtakingly wild to the brilliantly weird. And if it doesn't ring true, and your understanding of the south revolves around chicken shops and the occasional Reliant Robin, then this book is *definitely* for you. It will totally transform your perception of what lies south of the Thames (and it's not all wheeler-dealers and tennis tournaments).

London's north-south divide is almost as long-standing as the city itself, and runs as deep as the river that defines it. 'I don't go south of the river, love', once the standard response of north London cabbies tasked with dropping Dulwich-dwelling revellers home after a night out in Shoreditch, would sound preposterous today. In fact, these days you're just as likely to be partying south of the river, with Peckham and Brixton boasting some of the best dancefloors in the city (like Phonox, no.74).

We didn't make this book to prove that south London trumps north (we think both are equally brilliant) but if we had, we'd argue that the south has more green space; better views (Parliament Hill is great and all, but have you been up in the Battersea Power Station chimney, no.34?); and a far superior foodie scene, with more acclaimed restaurants, sustainable food markets and specialist delis than you can lob a plate of jellied eels at. And while we're at it, can north London boast grandparent/*Eastenders*-themed bars (no.69), multistorey-carparks-turned-community-arts-hubs (no.68), working 1950s ballrooms (no.70) or real-ale pubs inside old post offices (no.25)?

So go on, hop on the DLR... or the Overground... hell, hail a cab. And *do* go south of the river, love – you might discover something wonderful.

Emmy Watts
London, 2024

Emmy Watts has written seven other books in this series. She's lived on both sides of the river and, although Camden-based now, frequently ventures south in her eternal pursuit of fun places to drag her two young daughters, which she blogs about at bablands.com.

PERFECT WEEKEND

Friday night

Start the weekend with dinner and drinks in Brixton Village (no.33), before tootling over to Phonox (no.74) for DJs and dancing. If clubbing's not your thing, try one of Tate Modern's (no.52) arty Lates, followed by tacos at El Pastor (no.14) and a laid-back attempt at the Bermondsey Beer Mile (no.73).

Saturday morning

Get in line for a full fry-up at Milk (no.26) or coffee and pastries at Kapihan (no.28) (appetite dependent), then catch the latest exhibition at Studio Voltaire (no.62).

Saturday lunch

Hop over to Herne Hill before Lulu's (no.20) sells out of sandwiches and stock up on store-cupboard treats, then mosey across to Lowie (no.39) to peruse sustainable treasures. Then meander up to Brockwell Park and Lido (no.50) for a stroll and – if you're feeling brave – a revitalising dip.

Saturday afternoon

Swing by Lordship Lane's indie boutiques, ticking off Mons (no.7), Rye Books (no.31) and Meet Bernard (no.37). Grab something sweet from Eric's (no.23) and head towards Nunhead, stopping by Iyouall (no.30), ALKEMI (no.38) and The Nunhead Gardener (no.44). Finish with a cheeky pint at Skehans (no.71).

Saturday evening

Catch an early screening at Peckhamplex (no.61), then fill up on Persian sharing plates at Persepolis (no.17) or satisfying South Indian at Ganapati (no.13). In the summer months, Frank's (no.68) provides the drinks and the views, while Forza Wine (no.12) permits rooftop supping year-round.

Sunday brunch

Soothe sore heads with strong coffee and a restorative brunch at the South London Gallery (no.58) cafe, followed by a mooch around its light-filled gallery spaces. Alternatively, spend the morning at Beckenham Place Park (no.45), exploring ancient woodland, wild-swimming and sampling the delights of the weekly farmers' market.

Sunday afternoon

Head to Greenwich for a history lesson, courtesy of 'Britain's Sistine Chapel' (no.64), the home of Greenwich Mean Time and the world's largest maritime museum (no.55). Grab some savoury sustenance from Greenwich Market (no.24), not forgetting to pop by Dark Sugars (no.8) for sweet treats to take home.

Sunday evening

Jump on the DLR to Deptford and bid a fond farewell to the weekend with teapot cocktails and 'British tapas' at Little Nan's (no.69). Or, if that all sounds too kistch for your blood, put on your glad rags and slink down to Lyaness (no.67) in pursuit of some madcap mixology.

1

KUDU GRILL

Flame-cooked feasting

'Fire' is the theme of the Kudu collective's fourth instalment; not in the youth-vernacular sense (though that's true too), but by the fact that almost everything they serve has been grilled over a custom-built *braai* – South Africa's answer to the barbecue. And just as barbecues are best enjoyed al fresco, Kudu Grill's faultlessly charred dishes seem to taste all the richer for being devoured in the smart surrounds of this former Truman's pub – a cool and cosy space with stripped-back walls and green velvet booths. Peruse the menu over an SE15 Martini and a bowl of biltong (and then order a plate of treacly pork chops doused in monkey gland sauce anyway).

57 Nunhead Lane, SE15 3TR
Nearest station: Nunhead
kuducollective.com

2

BOROUGH MARKET

Famous foodie utopia

If you're looking for a foodie experience that will excite more than just your tastebuds, head straight for south London's oldest, biggest (and arguably best) food market. Occupying an atmospheric space beside Southwark Cathedral and sprawling in every direction under the railway lines, there has been a market here since at least the 12th century, with the current 4.5-acre site comprising more than 100 stalls, restaurants and shops. This epicurean wonderland dishes up everything from artisan bread to freshly shucked oysters, flavourful cured meats and magnificently stinky cheeses, with enough free samples that you could almost make a meal of these alone. Come here in search of speciality ingredients, gourmet gifts or a spot of top-notch street food.

SE1 9AL
Nearest station: London Bridge
boroughmarket.org.uk

3

THEO'S

Maximalist pizzas in minimalist surroundings

You'd be forgiven for strolling right past this corner-plot pizzeria with its whitewashed facade and simplistic signage. Thankfully there's nothing unremarkable about its pizzas, which come generously loaded and served in the form of crispy frittas (deep-fried pizzas), fat panuozzos (pizza sandwiches) and bubbly crusted classics. Menu regulars such as treacly aubergine and fiery nduja-topped pizzas are near-perfect, but it's the specials – crispy potatoes with lashings of pecorino fondue, creamed brussels sprouts encrusted with Cacio-cavallo – where Theo's really rises to the occasion. Help it all down with a glass of orange wine and a big dollop of their legendary chilli sauce.

2 Grove Lane, SE5 8SZ
Nearest station: Denmark Hill
Other location: Elephant & Castle
theospizzeria.com

4

PADELLA

Pasta paradise

If you're wondering whether Padella's queue length is directly proportional to the deliciousness of its pasta, you can rest assured it's worth the wait – and the inevitable carb coma. Perennially popular, the younger sibling of Tim Siadatan and Jordan Frieda's beloved Trullo is just as unfussy, offering up generous portions of freshly rolled, richly flavoured, reasonably priced pasta with remarkable efficiency given the compactness of the space. Pappardelle piled with rich beef shin ragu and velvety pici cacio e pepe are sell-out staples, but the seasonal specials are just as slurpable. Either way, best get in line.

6 Southwark Street, SE1 1TQ
Nearest station: London Bridge
Other location: Shoreditch
padella.co

5

THE CAMBERWELL ARMS

First-rate pub grub

A humdrum pub facade does very little to deter the hordes from this elegant restaurant, where stylishly stripped-back interiors allow Chef Director Mike Davies' culinary masterpieces to do the talking. If they did talk, Davies' dishes would probably be insufferable – such is the superiority of their ingredients, the polish of their presentation and their sheer deliciousness – but the pub's overarching vibe is one of humility, even despite its various accolades. Rouille-smothered mussels on toast, melt-in-the-mouth tempura pea pods and wickedly juicy pork crackling are just some of the unmissable pleasures on the seemingly mistitled 'Bar Snack' menu. The mains, while simpler, are just as decadent.

65 Camberwell Church Street, SE5 8TR
Nearest station: Denmark Hill
thecamberwellarms.co.uk

6

TOAD BAKERY

Dough of your dreams

You've got to eat a lot of substandard pastries before you find your devastatingly handsome cornbread croissant and ride off into the sunset (or at least hop on the 345) together. Beginning life in 2021 as a popup named Frog, Toad has all the components of a fairy-tale bakery: delightful staff, heavenly sourdough, robust coffee and an ever-changing assortment of freshly baked and wildly inventive sweet and savoury treats, from Boursin escargot pastries to giant Jaffa cakes. On the downside, everyone in Camberwell wants a slice of the action, so use your loaf and get here before the queues form.

44 Peckham Road, SE5 8PX
Nearest station: Denmark Hill
toadbakery.com

7

MONS CHEESEMONGERS

The big cheese

This shop stinks. And so it should! Founded in the 1960s by French cheesemaker Hubert Mons, today this (ahem) *mature* family business operates across four sites in south London, stocking around 190 mouthwatering varieties of British and continental cheese for an olfactory treat that needs to be whiffed to be believed. Whether you crave a corking Camembert, fancy a family fondue or have a yearning for a Yarg with a perfectly crumbly core, Mons has got every one of your cheese needs covered. Or, in 'queso' (sorry) cheesy overwhelm, head to one of their sporadic tasting events in search of your new favourite fromage.

153 Lordship Lane, SE22 8HX
Nearest station: East Dulwich
Other locations: Bermondsey, Borough Market
mons-cheese.co.uk

8

DARK SUGARS

Sweet dreams and ice creams

Willy Wonka ain't got nothing on Nyanga Fatou Mende, the Ghanaian-born confectioner behind this pleasure-seeker's paradise, famed for its generously loaded hot chocolates. You won't find candy flowers or lickable wallpaper here, but what you will find is arguably better: towering slabs of luxurious chocolate, wickedly rich truffles, mounds of velvety gelato and an aroma that will have you wondering if you've accidently plunged into a chocolate river. Deciding what to have is nigh on impossible (and the free samples won't aid your decision one bit), but the Classic Hot Chocolate is so-called for a reason – and the sinfully good Bailey's-spiked Irish Kiss is a necessary evil.

9 Nelson Road, SE10 9JB
Nearest station: Cutty Sark
darksugars.co.uk

9

NANDINE

Kurdish comfort food

Kurdish cuisine might lack representation in south London, but when the existing options are this enchanting we'll forgive the scarcity of choice. Headed up by chef Pary Baban, who fled her Iraqi hometown in the late 1980s during the Iraq-Kurdish conflict, this family-run kitchen is a heartfelt love note to Kurdistan; a place where the colours sing as loud as the flavours, and even a humble bowl of chips comes garlanded with pomegranate rubies. Nandine's rainbow-bright mezzes are legendary and few dishes hold the power to defeat a hangover like their hearty shakshuka, but it's the delectably flaky baklava that will leave the biggest impression – and probably the most mess down your front.

45 Camberwell Church Street, SE5 8TR
Nearest station: Denmark Hill
Other location: Vestry Road
nandine.co.uk

10

LEVAN

Electrifying modern bistro

Levan has a hell of a lot to live up to. Not only is the all-day dining spot the younger sibling of recently departed Brixton favourite Salon; it's named after Larry Levan, universally regarded as one of the greatest DJs who ever lived. Amazingly this place holds its own, serving up modern European bistronomy-inspired plates alongside a diverse assortment of natural wines, all to a pulsating disco soundtrack that would make Larry proud. Begin with a non-negotiable stack of comté fries before moving onto a dreamy bowl of caramelised celeriac tortellini, swiftly followed by buttery tarte tatin floating in a puddle of bay leaf custard. Sublime.

12-16 Blenheim Grove, SE15 4QL
Nearest station: Peckham Rye
levanlondon.co.uk

11

ARTUSI

Grade-A Italian

Classroom chairs and a daily-changing chalk-board menu lend this fuss-free dining room a decidedly schooly vibe, though thankfully the same can't be said about its food – even if it does serve as a robust lesson in Italian cuisine. Artusi isn't your average neighbourhood Italian and yet there's nothing showy about its menu, which spotlights seasonal vegetables, responsibly sourced meat and fish and pasta so fresh that sauce almost feels unnecessary. Gather the gang and order at least one of everything, plus extra desserts to take home (rest assured, the olive oil cake is about as far from a school pudding as you can get).

161 Bellenden Road, SE15 4DH
Nearest station: Peckham Rye
artusi.co.uk

12

FORZA WINE

Small plates, big views

In Italian, *forza* means 'force' or 'strength', but it's also used to describe the ability to face life's troubles. Coincidentally, an afternoon spent grazing and guzzling at this lively rooftop bar will completely dispel your worries – or at least offer a bit of escapism. Opened in 2019, the lofty offspring of nearby Italian Forza Win is a sunnier version of the original, with lighter bites and a bigger cocktail menu – not to mention magical views, which can be enjoyed whatever the season thanks to a glass-walled indoor space. Come 'forza' (natural) wine, stay for the crispy cauliflower fritti and the Lambrusco Spritz.

The Rooftop, 133a Rye Lane, SE15 4BQ
Nearest station: Peckham Rye
forzawine.com

13

GANAPATI

Enduring Indian restaurant

Restaurants rarely hang around for two decades in places like Peckham – let alone its residential backstreets – so this unassuming Indian kitchen must be doing something right. Founded by Claire Fisher in 2004 following a life-changing trip to southern India, Ganapati boasts an entire menu of Keralan-, Tamil- and Karnataka-inspired dishes done *very* right, from authentically buttery parathas to moreish battered street snacks, not to mention the flawless thalis and dosas that make up its epicurean lunch offer. Balmy days call for lassis on the banana tree-lined terrace, where you can daydream that you're in Bangalore… and not Bellenden Road.

38 Holly Grove, SE15 5DF
Nearest station: Peckham Rye
ganapatirestaurant.com

14

EL PASTOR

Taco walk on the wild side

Its name might literally translate as 'The Shepherd', but there's nothing sheepish about El Pastor, a fiery little taqueria under the railway arches beside Borough Market. The handle actually refers to the restaurant's signature taco – a Mexican evolution of the shawarma that marries smoky pork shoulder with charred, syrupy pineapple, brought to the region by Lebanese immigrants – but that's not to suggest ordering here is straightforward. You may well find yourself dithering between that, a cheeky tuna tostada and a beer-battered Baja taco (mercifully everything's relatively cheap, so you can probably stretch to all three). Temper all that heat with a cool mountain of guac and a frozen marg (or several).

7a Stoney Street, SE1 9AA
Nearest station: London Bridge
Other location: Soho
tacoselpastor.co.uk

15

THE
PECKHAM PELICAN

Understated arts cafe and bar

Elevated ceilings, swampy Chesterfields and a reliably well-chosen soundtrack make it easy to pass several hours in this low-key Peckham cafe, which moonlights as a lively bar. Positioned within paint-flicking distance of the South London Gallery and Camberwell College of Arts, this concrete retreat plays host to an enduringly arty crowd, while monthly exhibitions showcase fresh talent and frequent creative workshops generate even more. Fill your beak with their legendary bagels, which are baked on Brick Lane and given a south-of-the-river spin with fillings that span the sublime (the generously stacked halloumi and aubergine Camberwell Green) to the deliciously naff (the Peckham PB&J).

92 Peckham Road, SE15 5PY
Nearest station: Peckham Rye
thepeckhampelican.co.uk

16

GROVE LANE DELI

Sell-out eats and pantry treats

Delis are two a penny in London, but this dinky spot in Camberwell – where queues form before the shutters come up and patrons would sooner scoff their booty on the pavement outside than suffer the torture of waiting until they get home – is well worth saving your pounds for. While famed for its fluffy cinnamon buns, jaw-jamming sandwiches and malty Camberwell cookies, Grove Lane Deli should be just as lauded for its luxury pantry items, which include everything from Hadji Bey's tempting Turkish Delight to cans of Perelló olives the size of paint tins. Not your everyday lunch spot – even if you do find yourself there Wednesday through Sunday.

4a Grove Lane, SE5 8SY
Nearest station: Denmark Hill
grovelanedeli.com

GROVE LANE

DELI

Max 5
customers
at a time
please
Thank you

17

PERSEPOLIS

Characterful Persian cafe and deli

Ever inadvertently misplaced your keys? Let slip a secret? Opened a restaurant? This cult cafe might never have been intended as anything more than an (admittedly spectacularly well-stocked) Persian corner shop, but what began as an experimental few tables and a stove in the corner now regularly attracts snaking queues, and is one of South London's happiest accidents. Book ahead, BYOB and choose the ludicrously good-value feasting menu – a delectable line-up of crispy pakoras, honeyed paklavas and fragrant pilaf to share – before filling your boots with Iranian delicacies from the groaning grocery shelves.

28-30 Peckham High Street, SE15 5DT
Nearest station: Peckham Rye
foratasteofpersia.co.uk

18
GLADWELL'S DELI & GROCERY

Independent food hall

It's hard to imagine there was much pleasure to be had in this park-adjacent site back when it was a bank, but these days there's joy in every square foot, whether you're perusing indie produce or dropping by for brunch. A one-stop shop for locally produced cheese, wine, meat and greens, this lofty-ceilinged foodie mecca combines the convenience of a supermarket with the long-lost intimacy of the high street while showcasing numerous cult brands, from Wines Under the Bonnet to Cacklebean Eggs. Want more joy? Treat your mates to a private tasting in the atmospheric wine vault.

2 Camberwell Church Street, SE5 8QU
Nearest station: Denmark Hill
gladwells.co.uk

What's in Season....

Grapefruit
fi Lemons
rb
an Blood Oranges

Asparagus
Purple Sprouting
Perpetual Spinach
Spring Greens
Wild Garlic

19

JULIET'S QUALITY FOODS

Food for thought

'Worth the visit!' reads the cheery welcome sign on Juliet's doormat – a leftover from when the site was an Afro hair and beauty shop that still rings true. Set up by the former owners of Balham brunch favourite Milk (no.26), Juliet's is a stylishly serene spot that feels significantly more characterful than your average hipster caf, with a stripped-back frontage revealing glimpses of Tooting history and a mouthwatering menu filled with hearty comfort eats (including chilli-drenched chickpea farinata stuffed between thick slices of fermented potato bread, or a spicy shrimp burger that'll blow your head off). *Well* worth the visit, however long the tube journey.

110 Mitcham Road, SW17 9NG
Nearest station: Tooting Broadway
juliets.london

20
LULU'S

Cortados and cuvées

Not all superheroes wear capes. This local saviour, however, *does* lead a double life, keeping Herne Hill caffeinated by day and wined and dined by night, with luxury deli products thrown into the bargain. Lulu's is such a champ that you could pretty much stay all day, guzzling satisfyingly nutty cups of coffee and gorging on rustic, imaginatively filled sandwiches, nipping home for a siesta while it Supermans into a wine bar, and then returning for a Marmalade Martini and a plate of devilled eggs. You can even replenish your pantry while you're here, making this neighbourhood hero a veritable one-stop shop (plus it has a rather lovely orange-sherbet awning, which is *basically* a cape).

291 Railton Road, SE24 0JP
Nearest station: Herne Hill
lulus.london

Breakfast Martini 10
French 75 10
Suze & Tonic 8

Gilda 3ea
Cantabrian Anchovies 9
Culatello 9.5
Rosette de Lyon 8.5
House Focaccia 4
Preserved Lemon & Chilli 7.5

Leaves, Almonds & Mimolette 9.5
... & Pickled Mushrooms on Toast 14
Deviled Eggs & Trout Roe 15
... Celeriac, Beetroot, Egg Yolk & Horseradish 17
... Bacon, Morteau & Fennel 18

... Mushrooms, Jerusalem Artichoke 12
... Mushrooms, Betkswell & Chestnut 8.5

... Pot

21

SMOKE & SALT

Neighbourhood restaurant with cure-ious menu

It's rare that a supper club lasts long enough to become a fully-fledged restaurant, let alone one as great as Smoke & Salt, but then preservation *is* the MO of this modern British kitchen, where smoked and cured seasonal ingredients take centre-stage. Reassuringly straightforward, this pint-sized spot has recently done away with all but its sharing menu, a five- or seven-course feast comprising all manner of treats – smoked cod roe piped onto anchovy puffs, tempura chicory strewn with pickled cranberry jewels and a wickedly sticky date cake – all perfectly portioned and reasonably priced. A must-visit for any foodie worth their salt.

115 Tooting High Street, SW17 0SY
Nearest station: Tooting Broadway
smokeandsalt.com

22

CHATSWORTH BAKEHOUSE

Selling like hotcakes

You can thank social media for the queues that begin in the Victorian doorway of this dinky bakery every lunchtime and snake so far down Anerley Hill the end is often out of sight. Frequently dubbed London's best sandwich, its weekly-changing doorstop sarnie is so popular pre-orders sell out quicker than Glasto tickets, with regulars including bolstering bhaji butties and tangy patatas bravas piled on freshly baked focaccia. And while the queues *can* get a bit silly, there are definitely worse ways to spend a lunchtime than in pursuit of a toasted-marshmallow-topped cookie (or pretty much anything else this place sells, to be honest).

120a Anerley Road, SE19 2AN
Nearest station: Crystal Palace
chatsworthbakehouse.com

23
ERIC'S

The best thing since…

Anyone who remembers the croissants at Borough Market's erstwhile restaurant-turned-bakery Flor (sadly closed in 2022) will appreciate why there's always a queue outside this buttercup-yellow newbie, and why they should probably join it. Set up by Flor's former head baker Helen Evans, Eric's does a blooming trade in buttery morning buns, fabulously flaky pain au chocolat and something called 'porridge bread' that manages to be both immensely satisfying and embarrassingly moreish, along with seasonal specials that you'll blink once and miss. Sign up to the mailing list for details of workshops, pre-orders and other pressing pastry matters.

20 Upland Road, SE22 9EF
Nearest station: East Dulwich
ericslondon.com

24

GREENWICH MARKET

Indie bits and bites under a glass roof

A visit to Greenwich is glaringly incomplete without a browse around its buzzy 18th-century market, whose abundant shops and stalls cover everything from fashion and homeware to gourmet gifts and street food. Ferociously independent, the market offers an inimitable alternative to the usual high street fare, whether you're perusing London memorabilia at Liz Loves Liz's vintage sign stall, gorging on one of Pimp My Ramen's jaw-dislocating noodle burgers or indulging in a single-origin hot chocolate at Dark Sugars' flagship cocoa house (no.8). Come with an empty tote and an even emptier stomach.

SE10 9HZ
Nearest station: Cutty Sark
greenwichmarket.london

25

SYLVAN POST

You've got ale

Anyone who's spent significant time waiting in line at the Post Office will likely approve of this ex-delivery centre's transformation into a handsome public house. Here, eclectic furniture interspersed with original fittings, vintage Royal Mail ephemera, cosy booths and secret snug rooms offer a welcome departure from dreary commercial interiors, while nightmares of postal returns and snaking queues are long forgotten over local ales and craft beers, moreish light bites and seasonal pub grub. Head here on Sundays for the best Yorkshire puddings in the postcode, or Wednesdays for the fiendishly fun quiz.

Heron House, 24-28 Dartmouth Road, SE23 3XZ
Nearest station: Forest Hill
sylvanpost.co.uk

26

MILK

The cream of the cafes

Milk seems an appropriate name for a cafe that's invariably packed with infants, but don't let the rabble put you off your brunch. Alleviator of many a hangover in its 12-year reign, this trendy corner spot proves as popular with TikTokers as weary parents thanks to an arsenal of creative dishes that make your average avo toast look positively plebeian. Gather a gaggle of equally headachy mates (or some toddlers – frankly it doesn't matter) and order a heap of cheesy hash browns, Milk's Japanese-style twist on the fishfinger sandwich and probably the prettiest plate of pancakes you'll ever clap eyes on. A convincing case for never bothering with cereal again.

20 Bedford Hill, SW12 9RG
Nearest station: Balham
milk.london

27

BROWNS OF BROCKLEY

Attention-grabbing coffee shop

Possession of a jazzy mural probably isn't reason enough to choose one coffee shop over another, but Browns of Brockley's branded street art should at least stop you in your tracks long enough to get a whiff of its earthy aromas and go in search of their source. Queues tend to form but they move fast and the coffee, when it comes, is short, punchy, and best enjoyed with a substantial bake – be it a pastrami-stuffed Brick Lane bagel or a croissant the size of your head. They don't do loyalty cards, but their mural-matching merch offers an even better way to pledge your allegiance with a firm thumbs up.

5-6 Coulgate Street, SE4 2RW
Nearest station: Brockley
Other locations: East Dulwich, Forest Hill
brownsofbrockley.com

BROWNS OF BROCKLEY

28
KAPIHAN

Filipino coffee house

Anyone even vaguely familiar with Kapihan's irresistibly squishy bibingkas will have boundless compassion for the population of Battersea, who had to go without the sticky rice treats for more than a year while the cult Filipino cafe sought new premises. Now back in a bigger and arguably much better location just round the corner, the self-styled 'Original House of Kape't Tinapay' (literally meaning 'coffee and bread') has rendered our hearts even fonder and our tastebuds even keener for its gooey ube (purple yam) custard pies, fluffy spiced pandesal (bread roll) and those impossibly soft bibingkas. Wash it all down with a silky Spanish latte or a decadent Philippine hot chocolate. Bliss.

547 Battersea Park Road, SW11 3BL
Nearest station: Clapham Junction
kapihan.coffee

29

LUMBERJACK

Social-enterprise coffee spot

There's a welcome lack of plaid at this cosy cafe and deli, which is named more in reference to its sister organisation – bespoke furniture workshop Goldfinch – than because its clientele are particularly hairy. Part of local charity London Reclaimed, Lumberjack runs a pioneering trainee barista programme for 16-25s, as well as showcasing the reclaimed-wood tables, chairs and fittings constructed by Goldfinch's apprentice carpenters. While generously stuffed doorstop sarnies and full-bodied coffee should satisfy even the most voracious logger, the beautifully curated shop and deli are crammed with all manner of artisanal gifts and gourmet pantry treats – perfect for smuggling back to your cabin.

70 Camberwell Church Street, SE5 8QZ
Nearest station: Denmark Hill
wearelumberjack.co.uk

30

IYOUALL

Nordic nesting

When it comes to crowning south London's coolest neighbourhood, the jury's still out. But there's no debating the hippest place to buy your furniture. Set up in 2017 by the founders of local design consultancy IYA Studio, Iyouall is a Nordic furnishing fan's minimalist fantasy, showcasing everything from modular sofas to striking stationery from the cream of Scandi interiors brands (think Hay, Audo Copenhagen and String, to name a few). Come here for endless home inspiration and gifts for sophisticated friends.

48 East Dulwich Road, SE22 9AX
Nearest station: East Dulwich
Other location: Deptford
iyouall.com

31

RYE BOOKS

Bookworm wonderland

Behind this tiny black shop front you'll find portals to infinite universes, both real and imagined. Part of the East Dulwich landscape since 2011, Rye Books is in many ways the perfect indie bookstore, presenting old-world charm with a contemporary edge, and stocking a hand-picked selection of often unique and always thought-provoking titles. Settle down in the shop's tiny cafe with your new read and a cup of locally roasted Old Spike coffee. Should you manage to prise your nose out of your book, you'll find more reasons to linger in the form of regular author events and signings, chats with friendly owner Alistair and cuddles with his affable shop dog George.

47 North Cross Road, SE22 9ET
Nearest station: East Dulwich
ryebooks.co.uk

COFFEE
AMERICANO
FLAT WHITE
LATTE
CAPPUCCINO
ESPRESSO
OAT MILK
HIGH

OPEN HERE

OLD SPIKE
OLD SPIKE
OLD SPIKE

OLD SPIKE
OLD SPIKE
OLD SPIKE

IAIN BANKS
THE LITERATURE

is

LIFE DEATH
AND
EVERYTHING
IN BETWEEN
DON McCULLIN

ON MODERN LIVING

THE LIFE AND TIME
BENJAMIN
ZEPHANIAH
AUTOBIOGRAPHY

BENJAMIN ZEPHANIAH
BENJAMIN ZEPHANIAH

THE ORANGE
WENDY COPE

KAE
TEMPEST
DIVISIBLE BY ITSELF AND ONE

RYE
Match The Floor.

2024

THE LOST
POST

AVENGERS

HOW TO

THE
HOU
OF
RY

SUSAN

HAPPY
BIRTHDAY

HURRAH!

hurray!

CONGRA

32

FOREST

Enchanting plant emporium

This verdant Tardis absolutely lives up to its name. Here, wall-to-wall foliage spills out from the doorway, beckoning you into a rambling indoor wilderness populated by exotic houseplants. Hanging alluringly from the ceiling or sitting pretty in handcrafted planters alongside rustic gifts and vibrant blooms, cut flowers here are available as pick 'n' mix or in premade bouquets. Meanwhile, a packed programme of evening activities embracing everything from floristry and candle making to macramé and calligraphy offers endless motivation to head into the Forest after dark.

35 North Cross Road, SE22 9ET
Nearest station: East Dulwich
forest.london

33

BRIXTON VILLAGE

Vibrant independent shopping arcade

Once the thumping heart of Windrush-era Brixton, the previously derelict Granville Arcade was sensitively resuscitated – and, happily, listed – in the early 2000s. Though you'll find significantly fewer Afro-Caribbean businesses here today, the market remains one of London's most diverse, with more than 100 fiercely independent shops, cafes and bars trading across three covered avenues. You could easily spend a full day satisfying your soul with the Village's copious sights, fragrances and flavours, but those with less time should put hard-to-find ingredients from Nour Cash and Carry, diverse kids' books from Round Table and treasures from dedicated LGBT gift shop Philip Normal at the top of their shopping lists.

Coldharbour Lane, SW9 8PS
Nearest station: Brixton
brixtonvillage.com

34

BATTERSEA POWER STATION

Luxury shopping in legendary landmark

Pink Floyd probably didn't bank on Battersea's brick bastion reopening as a high-end shopping centre 45 years after it appeared on the cover of their *Animals* album with a pig soaring between its chimneys. Today's Battersea Power Station is too polished to feel rock 'n' roll, but it's still an excellent place to spend your money, whether you're stocking up on luxury beauty products at Space NK or enjoying a slap-up lunch at Bread Street Kitchen. And if that doesn't stoke your fire, make like the flying pig and reach brave new heights courtesy of an immersive chimney-lift experience offering 360-degree views of London. Powerful stuff.

Circus Road West, SW11 8DD
Nearest station: Battersea Power Station
batterseapowerstation.co.uk

35

LORENZO'S (RECORDS WANTED)

Community music store

Whether you're a record rookie or a vinyl veteran, this friendly neighbourhood record store has got your analogue music needs well and truly covered. Having proved a smash hit at Rye Lane's Sky Shopping City arcade, Lorenzo's shuffled over to Brockley Road in 2020, where it continues to offer an eclectic selection of releases old and new, without so much as a hint of vinyl snobbery. Owner Lorenzo Bandiera is so keen to make the medium accessible he's even hosted kids' workshops covering the basics of vinyl culture – so hip parents can rest assured that their little ones will soon be able to wax lyrical about experimental ambient or old-school house.

260a Brockley Road, SE4 2SF
Nearest station: Brockley
lorenzosrecordswanted.com

36

SEABASS CYCLES

Indie bike workshop

Whether you're a pro peddler or a riding rookie, no one is made to feel like a fish out of water at this friendly neighbourhood cycle shop, which offers servicing and repairs alongside custom builds for utility, gravel, touring and bikepacking. Named after a much-missed pet dog, Seabass is every bit the family affair, welcoming everything from wonky-wheeled pushchairs to child-seat setups and rear trailers into its lively workshop. Looking to step things up a gear? Keep an eye on their Instagram for exclusive collabs with other indie bike brands, as well as details of inclusive group rides and over-night adventures.

261 Rye Lane, SE15 4UR
Nearest station: Peckham Rye
seabasscycles.co.uk

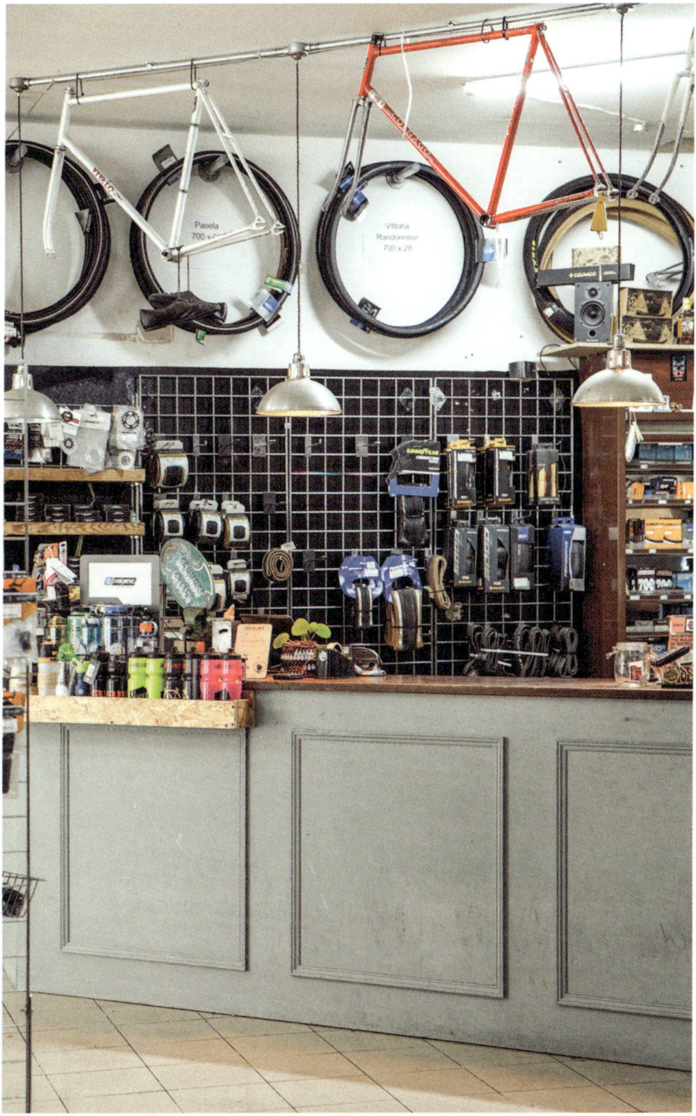
Pasela
Vittoria
Randonneur
700 x 28

37

MEET BERNARD

A stylish encounter

Southeast London first met Bernard back in 2006, when Ryan and Dani Chandler opened their first menswear store opposite Greenwich Market and immediately began turning heads. Nearly two decades, a Covid closure and a foray into womenswear later, what is now the area's oldest independent fashion shop currently exists as a pair of tempting boutiques in East Dulwich – one men's, one women's, both impossibly well curated with keep-forever treasures from Flower Mountain, Ganni, Howlin' and YMC, among copious other sustainable labels. If you've ever dreamt of digging through the wardrobes of the coolest guy and girl you know (and then stealing it all for yourself), this is your chance.

42 Lordship Lane, SE22 8HJ;
37 North Cross Road, SE22 9ET
Nearest station: East Dulwich
meetbernard.com

38

ALKEMI STORE

Elevating the everyday

There are lifestyle boutiques... and then there's
ALKEMI, a minimalist mini department store
that will make you want to throw out everything
you own, from your dinner plates to your dustpan,
and replace them with its dreamy wares (not that
eco-minded owner Jeane would approve). Quirky
kids' accessories, wooden toys, organic toiletries
and pared-back casualwear are just a few of the
many delights you'll want to toss in your tote,
with each item lovingly selected for its beauty and
functionality from an impeccable edit of mostly
Japanese, Korean and hyper-local brands. If only
life could always be this beautiful.

62 Nunhead Lane, SE15 3QE
Nearest station: Nunhead
Other location: Forest Hill
alkemistore.com

39

LOWIE

Sustainable style

Could it be the jazzy patterns, the promise of free lifetime repairs or the knowledge that every single garment has been ethically made by small-scale manufacturers? Whatever it is, there's something undeniably joyful about this sustainable womenswear store, where clothes are built for life and not just until the next trend rolls around. Indeed, Lowie's designs – and those of the shop's meticulously curated guest labels – seem to transcend fashion, offering flatteringly simple yet statement-making looks for eco-conscious women. Invest in a pair of their Turkish socks and a signature Fair Isle knit and you'll never be chilly again.

18 Half Moon Lane, SE24 9HU
Nearest station: Herne Hill
ilovelowie.com

40

LAMP/LDN

Spotlight on the home

This luxury lifestyle store might love lamps, but that's far from the extent of its remit. Set up when its founders' events business ground to a halt during lockdown, this peach-fronted boutique feels like a little ray of light: an unashamed celebration of the healing power of pretty things in ugly times. Beyond the scalloped window shades, you'll find everything from candles to cushions and books to bubble bath – alongside custom lampshades in a vast array of fabrics. Whether you're perusing for presents or just indulging your homeware habit, few boutiques shine brighter.

20b Maxted Road, SE15 4LF
Nearest station: Peckham Rye
lamplondonhome.com

41

KIRKDALE BOOKSHOP

Community literary hub

As is often the case with indie bookshops that pre-date the advent of digital media, this labyrinthine spot has evolved into something much more than a humble bookstore. A Sydenham linchpin since 1966, this turquoise-fronted treasure is as fabled for its community literary events as its books, with regular launches, a children's story time, an LGBTQIA+ book club and even a Christmas party for staff and customers alike. Or should you prefer to devour your literature in a more solitary fashion, take a seat in the tranquil backroom and lose yourself between the pages of a thrilling new release or pre-loved classic. Either way, this is definitely one to bookmark.

272 Kirkdale, SE26 4RS
Nearest station: Sydenham
kirkdalebookshop.com

42

GENTLY

Family lifestyle stores

The hip and child-hampered of southeast London let out a collective squeal of delight when Gently Elephant branched into homeware in 2017 – five whole years after the cherished kids' shoe and toy specialist flung open its doors on Brockley Road. These days this indie mini-chain is probably better known for its grown-up treats, boasting three lifestyle stores peddling everything from elegant Japanese stationery and Danish kitchenware to luxe beauty products and gifts you'll want to keep yourself – though there's still nowhere we'd rather kit out our kids' feet. Be warned though, this place might be Gently by name, but it'll be downright ruthless on your pocket.

405 Brockley Road, London SE4 2PH
Nearest station: Crofton Park
Other locations: Ladywell, Brockley, Harefield
gentlyelephant.co.uk

43

LASSCO

Architectural treasure chest

Does the term 'salvage' bring to mind abandoned cars and yards piled high with junk? Renovate your thinking with a trip to this architectural reclamation showroom, whose exceptional finds span chimneypieces and flooring to the kitchen sink, all displayed against the suitably faded grandeur of a crumbling Palladian mansion. While stock varies wildly, it's reliably fascinating – and consistently pricy. When you've finished hunting for relics (or just a little inspiration), indulge your tastebuds at the on-site restaurant, where appropriately nostalgic dishes, from loaded devilled eggs to revamped rice pudding, are magicked up by chef Jackson Boxer (grandson of cookbook legend Arabella, speaking of treasures...).

30 Wandsworth Road, SW8 2LG
Nearest station: Vauxhall
lassco.co.uk

44

THE NUNHEAD GARDENER

Horticultural healing

Maybe it's just our collective scarcity of personal outdoor space, but London's garden centres hit different. This one, which occupies the labyrinthine railway arches beside Nunhead station, is particularly bewitching, having been set up by ex-corporate couple Peter Milne and Alejandro Beltran to give urban gardeners not just somewhere to buy compost, but a place to explore and unwind, surrounded by lush greenery. In among the foliage, you'll find all manner of stylish pots, planters and gardening accessories, alongside a small selection of high-end homewares and tasteful greetings cards. Head here when your garden's in need of a little TLC – or even just when you are.

1a Oakdale Road, SE15 3BW
Nearest station: Nunhead
Other locations: Camberwell, Elephant & Castle, Mayfair
thenunheadgardener.com

OUTDOORS

45

BECKENHAM PLACE PARK

Stately green space with swimming lake (and more)

Once a faded remnant of Palladian splendour, Lewisham's largest green space was returned to its former glory in 2019 following a three-year restoration that saw the one-time gentleman's seat and its grounds relaunched as a verdant leisure destination. Home to London's first purpose-built swimming lake, fashioned from an original Georgian water feature, this resplendent 237-acre site also boasts ancient woodland and a large BMX track, while its hauntingly beautiful mansion hosts community events, a cosy cafe, a resident sewing school and a characterful vintage shop. Head down on Sundays to sample street eats and pantry treats, courtesy of the vibrant farmers' market.

Beckenham Hill Road, BR3 1SY
Nearest station: Beckenham Hill
beckenhamplacepark.com

46

CRYSTAL PALACE PARK

Dinosaurs and dead ends

The gleaming glass giant that gave the area its name might be long gone, but this 200-acre park remains a treasured monument to Victoriana, famed as much for Benjamin Waterhouse Hawkins' anatomically incorrect dinosaur sculptures as for the erstwhile exhibition hall. As well as Hawkins' beloved relics, the site is home to a brilliantly bewildering maze and a magnificent Italian subway that once gave access to the palace – both beautifully preserved monuments to the park's 19th century heyday. A spacious branch of beloved local brunch chain Brown and Green is a welcome 21st-century addition – the masala breakfast is a must-try.

Thicket Road, SE19 2GA
Nearest station: Crystal Palace
crystalpalaceparktrust.org

47

RICHMOND PARK

Ian Dury, rhododendrons and 600 deer

Londoners have been flocking to Richmond Park in pursuit of rural refuge ever since Charles I fled a plague outbreak in the capital and established the site as a deer-hunting park. Four centuries later, little has changed – though the establishment of Victorian floral glory the Isabella Plantation is perhaps the most notable modification – and the descendants of the Stuart king's herd still roam free through 2,500 acres. You're free to do the same, and the park's western edge is a great place to start, with the elegant Pembroke Lodge cafe, Ian Dury's musical memorial bench and city-wide views from King Henry's Mound all within moments of each other.

TW10 5HS
Nearest station: Richmond
royalparks.org.uk/visit/parks/richmond-park

48

BATTERSEA PARK

Invigorating urban oasis

With its exhilarating Segway trail and Go Ape treetop adventure, this 200-acre green space might offer more thrills than most, but there's still boundless tranquillity to be found beneath its 4,000 trees. Particularly popular with families, the park is also home to a delightful children's zoo and an epic playground that's beloved by tots up to teens, while the hireable recumbent bikes and pedalos are invariably commandeered by kids. Forgo the picnic and head to the lake-adjacent Pear Tree Cafe instead, where you can recover from your excitement with an elegant brunch served up by ex-Petersham Nurseries chefs.

49

THAMES PATH WALK

South Bank perambulation

Skyscrapers, ships and monumental sculpture. There's no scarcity of spectacle on this exhilarating riverside walk – a 30-mile jaunt that stretches from picturesque Teddington Lock in the west to the gleaming Thames Barrier in the east, via countless urban wonders. Part of a much longer trail that extends out to the Cotswolds and the Thames Estuary, this dot-to-dot of London landmarks is best tackled in bitesize chunks, with well-placed boozers primed for recuperative pints along the way (Twickenham's White Swan and Wapping's Prospect of Whitby are particular favourites), and plenty else to tempt you off course, from high-end shopping destinations to world-class museums.

Teddington Lock, TW11 9NG
to Thames Barrier, E16 2EQ
www.nationaltrail.co.uk/en_GB/trails/thames-path

50

BROCKWELL PARK & LIDO

Family-friendly green space with Art Deco pool

Brockwell Park is *brilliant* for kids, with its tiny trains, paddling pools and a huge three-part playground designed to appeal to all ages, but it's just as great for grown-ups, too. Meander the tranquil walled flower garden and explore the abundant sports facilities, including the iconic 1930s lido (unheated) with its stoic posse of regulars. Once you've worked up a sweat swimming laps, tearing up the BMX track or just chasing after your kids, head to celebrated sourdough pizza and craft beer spot Four Hundred Rabbits for a fluffy-crusted margherita and a glass of something 'hoppy'.

Dulwich Road, SE24 0PA
Nearest station: Herne Hill
lambeth.gov.uk/parks/brockwell-park

51

NUNHEAD CEMETERY

Unkempt burial ground with gothic monuments

This rambling wilderness might have been purchased for £1 (by Southwark Council in 1975, following its abandonment by its previous owners), but its calmative powers are priceless. Perhaps the least famous of London's so-called Magnificent Seven cemeteries, this seemingly forgotten secret is closely tended by local volunteers, whose vital work includes preserving the magical views of St Paul's Cathedral via a cut-through in the trees. Memorials to a drowned local scout troop and the brother of troubled poet Charlotte Mew feel particularly poignant, but the atmosphere is more uplifting than gloomy, with magnificent Victorian tombstones, intertwining trees and undisturbed wildlife affording a bewitching backdrop for serene strolls.

Linden Grove, SE15 3LP
Nearest station: Nunhead
fonc.org.uk

52

TATE MODERN

Cathedral of contemporary art

What links a 30-foot spider, a 167-metre crack in the floor and an army of airborne jellyfish? They'd all incite a mass exodus in most scenarios, but at Tate Modern they've at times each been a Turbine Hall commission – all dreamt up for the iconic five-storey space by some of the biggest names in art. But this exciting annual commission is far from the extent of the gallery's offer, which spans illuminating permanent displays, lavish retrospectives and imaginative family workshops sure to inspire a new generation of art enthusiasts (at least, provided there are no 30-foot spiders involved).

Bankside, SE1 9TG
Nearest station: Blackfriars
tate.org.uk

53

SHAKESPEARE'S GLOBE

Open-air playhouse

All the world's a stage, but when it comes to the works of Shakespeare there's only one place to experience them. Built just moments from the original Globe, this faithful reconstruction has staged dazzling productions of every one of the Bard's plays over its 25-year run, from traditional adaptations to modern reinventions and everything in between. Famed for its audience participation, this timber-framed, thatch-roofed amphitheatre offers the ultimate immersive theatre experience, with family-friendly performances and tickets for as little as £5 for those who are happy to stand. The only question is what to see – or not to see.

21 New Globe Walk, SE1 9DT
Nearest station: London Bridge
shakespearesglobe.com

54

IMPERIAL WAR MUSEUM

Sobering stories of wartime experience

The history of modern conflict might not make for particularly cheerful viewing, but its vital lessons are always engagingly presented at this impressive museum. Whether your teen is revising trench warfare or your ten-year-old is riveted by the Blitz, IWM's expansive displays promise to captivate the whole family, sensitively combining interactive installations and audio-visual testimonies with millions of artefacts and photographs to highlight the human experience of war. The haunting Holocaust Galleries should be compulsory viewing for over-14s, while younger ones will really 'get into' the WWI Galleries' immersive trench experience.

Lambeth Road, SE1 6HZ
Nearest station: Lambeth North
iwm.org.uk

55

ROYAL MUSEUMS GREENWICH

Nautical museums on world heritage site

Greenwich's proud maritime history comes majestically to the fore at this quartet of iconic museums: the imposing Royal Observatory, the Queen's House (a former seamen's hospital), historic sailing ship, the Cutty Sark and the world's oldest and largest maritime museum. Chances to straddle two hemispheres on the Prime Meridian line, witness one of the world's largest refracting telescopes and marvel at the jacket Admiral Nelson died in are mere drops in the museums' vast ocean of delights, but rookie sailors should report straight for duty at the NMM immersive Ahoy! Play Area or its ambitious pirate-themed playground.

Nearest station: Cutty Sark, Greenwich
rmg.co.uk

56

HORNIMAN MUSEUM AND GARDENS

Eclectic museum full of quirky specimens

You'll find all creatures great, small and stuffed at this characterful museum, a south London family favourite that grew from founder Frederick John Horniman's mammoth collection of natural history specimens. The oddly endearing taxidermy collection headed up by the infamous overstuffed walrus is closed for refurb until 2026, but it's still worth visiting the Art Nouveau-inspired building to explore the small but popular aquarium and inspiring programme of creative children's exhibitions. The 16 acres of gardens are also home to an animal walk and butterfly house, plus breathtaking views across London and an outdoor cafe kiosk that makes for an unbeatable picnic spot.

100 London Road, SE23 3PQ
Nearest station: Forest Hill
horniman.ac.uk

57

WHITE CUBE

Bermondsey bulwark known for trailblazing shows

Named for its interior aesthetic rather than its facade, this breathtaking contemporary art space never fails to deliver drama with its world-class exhibitions. Gaining notoriety by hosting many YBA shows in the 1990s, White Cube continues to serve up some of the capital's most sensational art experiences, from physiological encounters with Antony Gormley's labyrinthine sculptures to moving confrontations with Anselm Kiefer's apocalyptic installations. Best of all, no matter how big the name, admission is always free, whether you're exploring Ann Veronica Janssen's dreamscapes or getting lost in Julie Mehretu's canvases.

144-152 Bermondsey Street, SE1 3TQ
Nearest station: London Bridge
whitecube.com

58

SOUTH LONDON GALLERY

Pioneering contemporary art space

Its eponymy says a lot about this spectacular art gallery, which occupies a pair of architecturally distinct yet equally impressive buildings on opposite sides of Peckham Road. Dedicated to contemporary work since the 1990s, SLG has hosted many significant art moments in the last couple of decades, from Tracey Emin's infamous *Everyone I Have Ever Slept With* to Thomas Hirschhorn's post-apocalyptic *In-Between*. Kick off your art journey at the light-filled Fire Station space and finish it off with melt-in-the-mouth pastries at South London Louie – brunch favourite Louie Louie's stylish SLG outpost.

65 Peckham Road, SE5 8UH
Nearest station: Queens Road Peckham, Denmark Hill
southlondongallery.org

59

COPELAND PARK
& BUSSEY BUILDING

Hip cultural complex with shops and studios

Anyone heading to Copeland Park in search of a
verdant savannah may be disappointed on arrival
at this motley assortment of industrial buildings.
Have a poke around, though, and all is forgiven.
Home to the legendary South London Soul Train,
the Bussey Building is a failsafe destination for
getting your groove on, but there's plenty to do here
in daylight hours, too. From indie stores peddling
tasteful stationery and homeware (The Completist,
Etc.) and vintage vinyl (Peckham Soul, Inverted
Audio) to galleries and boutique gyms, not to mention the cherry-on-the-top summertime rooftop
bar, this former cricket bat factory is a bricks-and-
concrete embodiment of Peckham's creative spirit.

133 Copeland Road, SE15 3SN
Nearest station: Peckham Rye
copelandpark.com

60
SOUTHBANK CENTRE
Iconic riverside arts hub

The South Bank's Brutalist arts complex began life
as the triumphant Festival of Britain in 1951 – and
the party hasn't stopped since. Home to six resident
orchestras, this lively landmark is best known for
its classical concerts, though there's infinitely more
to its programme, with 5,000 events staged across
three performance venues every year. Trailblazing
theatre, masterclasses with prominent writers and
a wildly popular annual children's festival are just
the tip of this cultural iceberg, with much of it
free to enjoy. Meanwhile, the cavernous Hayward
Gallery has a knack for securing the capital's
most electrifying art exhibitions, with memorable
moments including Jeremy Deller's snack bar and
Gelitin's rooftop boating lake.

Belvedere Road, SE1 8XX
Nearest station: Waterloo
southbankcentre.co.uk

61

PECKHAMPLEX

The big screen on a budget

In a city where you can easily pay £20 to catch the latest release, a cinema that charges little more than a fiver a ticket sounds like the stuff of silver-screen fantasy. Formerly the Peckham Multiplex, this six-screen Shangri-La shows everything from art-house flicks to big-budget blockbusters in a space that reflects the price – simple and reminiscent of the 1990s, complete with vibrant decor, nostalgic pick 'n' mix and sticky floors. You won't find reclining sofas or movie-themed cocktails here, but the accessible screenings, niche film festivals and friendly staff are all pretty excellent bonus features.

95a Rye Lane, SE15 4ST
Nearest station: Peckham Rye
peckhamplex.london

62

STUDIO VOLTAIRE

Feisty indie arts centre

The artist-designed toilets are reason enough to make the pilgrimage to this recently refurbished Clapham gallery – and they're not even the best thing about the space, which inhabits a Victorian former mission hall close to the eastern tip of the Common. Since moving to its current site in 1999, Studio Voltaire has hosted everything from Ruth Ewan's living aviary to a retrospective of nudist performance-art group Neo Naturists, as well as large-scale installations including a monumental pink pyramid by Joanne Tatham and Tom O'Sullivan. Don't depart without snaffling an arty souvenir from the terrific gift shop, grabbing lunch in the resident-run cafe and spending a penny in *that* toilet.

1a Nelsons Row, SW4 7JR
Nearest station: Clapham Common
studiovoltaire.org

63

ELTHAM PALACE AND GARDENS

Stylish 1930s mansion with medieval annexe

What do you get when you cross a medieval palace with an Art Deco mansion? It may sound like the setup for a joke, but Eltham Palace's amalgam of architectural styles makes for a seriously unique day out. At various points the home of both Henry VIII and millionaire philanthropists Stephen and Virginia Courtauld (not forgetting their pet lemur, who had its own central-heated room), this extraordinary property is a must-see for Tudor fanatics and modern architecture mavens alike, offering fascinating opportunities to delve into the Courtaulds' eccentric private lives – and the small matter of almost a thousand years of history.

Court Yard, SE9 5QE
Nearest station: Eltham, Mottingham
english-heritage.org.uk/visit/places/
eltham-palace-and-gardens

64

OLD ROYAL NAVAL COLLEGE

Architectural gem with dramatic interior

Hear 'Greenwich', and you're likely already picturing the iconic exterior of Sir Christopher Wren's twin-domed masterpiece – but this seamen's-hospital-turned-naval-college is more than just a pretty facade. Often touted as Britain's answer to the Sistine Chapel, its spectacular Painted Hall warrants at least an hour spent gazing at the ceiling from the comfort of one of its day beds, while the site of Admiral Nelson's lying-in-state and the richly decorated chapel are just as unmissable. Visiting with kids? Call ahead to check the opening times of the immaculately preserved (and still-in-use) Victorian skittle alley.

SE10 9NN
Nearest station: Cutty Sark
ornc.org

65

POLKA THEATRE

Putting kids centre-stage

Polka raised the curtain on its dramatic reno-
vation in 2021, unveiling a bigger and infinitely
more magical new space befitting of the UK's first
dedicated children's theatre. As well as installing
a flexible Adventure Theatre for little ones, the
playful new Polka has undergone quite the scene
change, with wildly imaginative new indoor and
outdoor playscapes, and a kid-friendly cafe for
post-show chomping. Performances cater to babies
all the way up to pre-teens and are accompanied by
a lively programme of drama workshops and masterclasses. All in all, a mighty tough act to follow.

240 The Broadway, SW19 1SB
Nearest station: South Wimbledon
polkatheatre.com

66

BFI

Queen of the screens

If you think nothing beats seeing a film on the big screen, try the BFI IMAX – covering a vast 512.8 square metres – for size. Part of the institute's South Bank complex, this is the cinema to end all cinemas, showing new releases alongside cult classics, immersive documentaries and special-guest screenings in godly proportions. When the credits roll, take a short stroll over the subway to the riverside location, BFI Southbank, for a post-picture refuel in one of the buzzy bars; make it a movie marathon with another flick in one of the three additional screens – with special seasons offering deep dives into niche genres or the work of particular directors; or take a trip down memory lane in the dazzling Mediatheque archive.

Belvedere Road, SE1 8XT
Nearest station: Waterloo
bfi.org.uk

67

LYANESS

Experimental cocktails in swanky space

Forget piña coladas and Sex on the Beach – this audacious cocktail bar is much more likely to serve up something deliciously unexpected. Cricket-cordial suffused mezcals and petrified-poo martinis might sound like the sort of concoctions you'd resort to imbibing on a desert island, but this riverside spot is less castaway, more cruise liner with its plush teal banquettes and green marble bar (the latter a hand-me-down from owner Mr Lyan's Dandelyan, considered the best bar in the world before it closed). The drinks menu is fairly inscrutable but that's all part of the fun, and whether you plump for a refreshing Safety Frappé or a floral Doc Americano, you'll be far from disappointed.

20 Upper Ground, SE1 9PD
Nearest station: Southwark
lyaness.com

68

BOLD TENDENCIES
& FRANK'S CAFE

Cultural hub and summertime rooftop bar

Only in Peckham could a sad multistorey carpark metamorphose into one of London's most exciting public spaces, replete with a rooftop bar, permanent artworks from the likes of Richard Wentworth and Jenny Holzer and the capital's best-known bubblegum-pink staircase. The first architectural project from not-for-profit arts organisation Bold Tendencies, Frank's Cafe is only open for five months of the year, emerging from its winter hibernation every May with a tempting cocktail and light-bites menu plus an annual sculpture show and live programme (also commissioned by Bold Tendencies).

95a Rye Lane, SE15 4ST
Nearest station: Peckham Rye

69
LITTLE NAN'S BAR

Kitsch cocktail bar

Pat Butcher might seem an unlikely muse for a multi-award-winning cocktail bar, but any pre-conceptions are best left at the door of this fabled spot, where the cocktails come in teapots and the furniture once graced owner Tristan's late nan's sitting room. Loud, leopard-printed and unabashedly tawdry, this wildly popular spot is a tongue-in-cheek celebration of community, *faaamilly* and *Eastenders*. So, clip on your best chandelier earrings, grab a settee and fill your boots with brilliantly beige 'teacup tapas' (onion rings, fish fingers, chicken strips) and as many Alfie Moon-themed cocktails as you like – after all, you ain't my muvva!

Deptford Market Yard, SE8 4BX
Nearest station: Deptford
littlenans.co.uk

70

RIVOLI BALLROOM

Old-fashioned knees-ups in '50s dance hall

If the illuminated promise of 'dancing tonight' isn't enough to lure you beyond the Rivoli's Art Deco-inspired facade, perhaps the idea of shaking a leg in London's oldest original ballroom is. Originally built as a cinema, this Grade II-listed venue is, admittedly, not *all* about the dancing (its chandelier-lit, flock-wallpapered dance hall also accommodates movie nights, film shoots and music videos), but there are ample chances to boogie, if that's your jam, from '90s nights to reggae revelries and jive parties to soul shindigs. Vintage attire encouraged.

350 Brockley Road, SE4 2BY
Nearest station: Crofton Park
rivoliballroom.com

71
SKEHANS

Easy-going Irish pub

What makes a cracking pub? Or should that be a *craic*-ing pub? Indeed, this family-owned Irish indie, which regularly tops London's 'best boozer' lists, attributes much of its popularity to its sense of fun – something that appears to be the only common denominator among its diverse throng of punters. Whether you're here for the tense weekly pub quiz, near-nightly live music sets, a big bowl of pad thai in the garden restaurant or just a quiet pint by the fire, there are always good times (and Guinness) on tap at Skehans.

1 Kitto Road, SE14 5TW
Nearest station: Nunhead
skehans.com

72

PECKHAM CELLARS

Corking good wine bar

Food, wine and a real good time: that's the philosophy behind this laid-back wine bar and restaurant, which occupies a remarkably bright and un-cellar-like spot on the corner of Peckham's Queen's Road. The name, of course, refers to its vast arsenal of natural wines, which all look tempting but could very easily defeat you if the staff weren't so keen to recommend the *exact* bottle to perfectly complement your food, whether it's tempura purple broccoli or braised octopus. Small plates not your idea of a good time? Try one of their legendary parties instead.

125 Queen's Road, SE15 2ND
Nearest station: Queen's Road Peckham
peckhamcellars.co.uk

73

THE BERMONDSEY BEER MILE

Artisanal taproom trail

When is a pub crawl not a pub crawl? While there's no official line-up, most iterations of the Bermondsey Beer Mile don't incorporate traditional pubs. Instead, you'll find just shy of 20 indie breweries and taprooms lined up in a row for your hop-hopping pleasure, stretching from foodie mecca Maltby Street Market to Fourpure's massive South Bermondsey brewery (or vice versa, depending on how hungry you are). Follow the arches and you can't go far wrong, but be sure to include The Barrel Project for sours, Cloudwater for the best blurry pale ales and IPAs, Craft Beer Junction for offbeat flavours and Kanpai for a cheeky sake to mix things up.

www.bermondsey-beer-mile.co.uk

74

PHONOX

Atmospheric nightclub with diverse programme

This esteemed nightspot rose like a phoenix (or, indeed, a Phonox) from the ashes of predecessor Plan B in 2016 and quickly became every south London reveller's plan A for a banging night out. A state-of-the-art sound system, reasonable ticket prices and a seriously laid-back vibe (no phones on the dancefloor) have ensured the enduring popularity of this 450-cap industrial venue. Look out for the legendary 'Fridays at Phonox' residencies – where big-name DJs from Call Super to Romare take the reins for four nights a month, programming night-long sets with special guests – or pop in on a Sunday afternoon for a more chilled-out, intimate soundtrack.

418 Brixton Road, SW9 7AY
Nearest station: Brixton
phonox.co.uk

75

BERMONDS LOCKE

Affordable aparthotel

Fancy living like a London Bridge local for a few days (or even up to a year)? Designed to shake up the traditional guesthouse experience, Locke's only south London aparthotel combines the convenience of a hotel with the privacy of an apartment, offering restful studios and suites complete with sofas and kitchenettes, all at very un-SE1 prices. Downstairs, the sunny coworking space encourages maximum productivity, with caffeine boosts courtesy of the trendy in-house coffee bar and endless foodie options on the doorstep, with Maltby Street Market and Bermondsey Street both so close you can almost smell them. On second thoughts, maybe we'll just stay forever…

157 Tower Bridge Road, SE1 3LW
Nearest station: London Bridge
lockeliving.com

76

THE HOXTON

Hip hotel close to the South Bank

Its opulent interiors might take their cue from the factories that once dominated the Southwark skyline, but the Hoxton chain's third London instalment still feels just like home. Set across 13 storeys, this laid-back haven offers guests a fully customisable stay, whether you settle on a spacious Biggy or cosy Shoebox room, go all out with oysters and martinis at the rooftop restaurant or keep it (relatively) lowkey with beer and burgers in the ground-floor brasserie. You can even opt to have breakfast delivered to your door, making venturing out of your room at all completely non-compulsory (though if you do fancy a stroll, be sure to check out neighbouring Tate Modern – another striking reminder of the area's industrial past).

40 Blackfriars Road, SE1 8NY
Nearest station: Southwark
thehoxton.com

IMAGE CREDITS

An Opinionated Guide to South London
First edition

Published in 2024 by Hoxton Mini Press, London
Copyright © Hoxton Mini Press 2024. All rights reserved.

Text by Emmy Watts
Editing by Florence Ward
Design and production by Richard Mason
Proofreading by Zoë Jellicoe
Editorial support by Leona Crawford

With thanks to Matthew Young for initial series design.

Please note: we recommend checking the websites listed for each
entry before you visit for the latest information on price, opening times
and pre-booking requirements.

The right of Emmy Watts to be identified as the creator of this Work
has been asserted under the Copyright, Designs and Patents Act 1988.

Thank you to all of the individuals and institutions who have provided images
and arranged permissions. While every effort has been made to trace the present
copyright holders we apologise in advance for any unintentional omission or error,
and would be pleased to insert the appropriate acknowledgement in any
subsequent edition.

A CIP catalogue record for this book is available from the British Library.

ISBN: 978-1-914314-59-9

Printed and bound by OZGraf, Poland

Hoxton Mini Press is an environmentally conscious publisher, committed
to offsetting our carbon footprint. This book is 100 per cent carbon compensated,
with offset purchased from Stand For Trees.

Every time you order from our website, we plant a tree:
www.hoxtonminipress.com

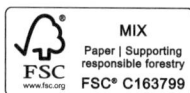

MIX
Paper | Supporting
responsible forestry
FSC® C163799

Selected opinionated guides in the series:

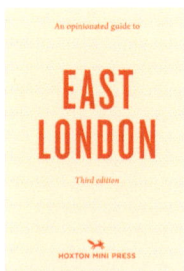

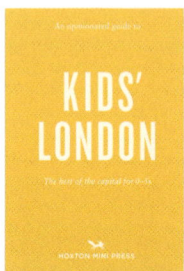

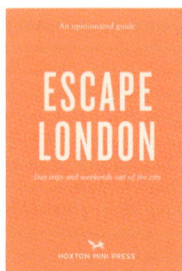

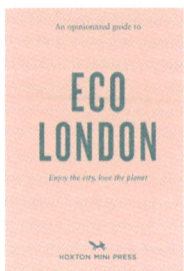

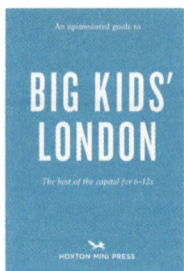

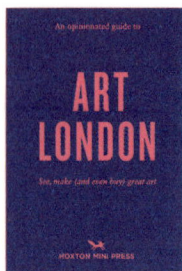

An opinionated guide to

EAST LONDON

Third edition

HOXTON MINI PRESS

An opinionated guide to

LONDON ARCHITECTURE

HOXTON MINI PRESS

An opinionated guide to

LONDON GREEN SPACES

HOXTON MINI PRESS

An opinionated guide to

INDEPENDENT LONDON

The Capital's Best Small Shops

HOXTON MINI PRESS

An opinionated guide to

KIDS' LONDON

The best of the capital for 0-5s

HOXTON MINI PRESS

An opinionated guide

ESCAPE LONDON

Day trips and weekends out of the city

HOXTON MINI PRESS

An opinionated guide to

ECO LONDON

Enjoy the city, love the planet

HOXTON MINI PRESS

An opinionated guide to

BIG KIDS' LONDON

The best of the capital for 6-12s

HOXTON MINI PRESS

An opinionated guide to

ART LONDON

See, make (and even buy) great art

HOXTON MINI PRESS

For more go to www.hoxtonminipress.com

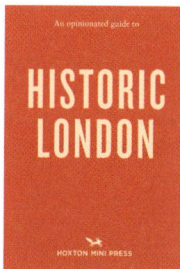

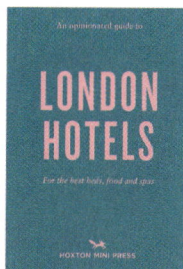

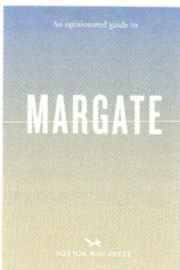

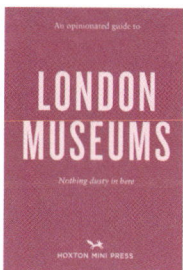

An opinionated guide to
VEGAN LONDON
Second edition

HOXTON MINI PRESS

An opinionated guide to
FREE LONDON
Enjoy the capital without the cash

HOXTON MINI PRESS

An opinionated guide to
LONDON DELIS

HOXTON MINI PRESS

An opinionated guide to
QUEER LONDON

HOXTON MINI PRESS

An opinionated guide to
HISTORIC LONDON

HOXTON MINI PRESS

An opinionated guide to
LONDON HOTELS
For the best beds, food and spas

HOXTON MINI PRESS

An opinionated guide to
CYCLE LONDON

HOXTON MINI PRESS

An opinionated guide to
MARGATE

HOXTON MINI PRESS

An opinionated guide to
LONDON MUSEUMS
Nothing dusty in here

HOXTON MINI PRESS

INDEX